Consequences

This book belongs to

_____

Written by Stephen Barnett
Illustrated by Rosie Brooks

Contents

About this book

This book shows children that love for a pet means responsibility and trying to do something in life is more important than being successful in it.

Consequences

I wanted to have a pet of my own. My parents weren't so sure.
'Who will look after the little animal?' asked my mother. 'Young animals need lots of care. You would have to feed it and also clean it regularly. Are you sure you can do all this?'

'Yes! Yes! Of course!' I said. 'It won't be a problem. I will spend all my time with it and do everything that's needed.'
'Hmmm, it's a big responsibility, you know. Let me talk to your father about it and then we will decide.'

Two days later my parents announced that I could have a pet.
'I think I'll have a kitten,' I said, excitedly. The next day we found someone whose cat had given birth to two kittens. I choose the kitten which was of black and white colour. I called it 'Tiger'.

The next few days were full of fun, carrying
Tiger around the house, feeding it, stroking
its fur and playing with it. I was happy to do
everything the kitten needed.

A week passed in this manner. And then I starting to think about the other things I usually did. 'You can do all the things that you did earlier. But just remember that the kitten must come first as you are responsible for it,' said mother.

'I'll remember,' I said.

One weekend, my friend Anna invited me to play at her house. On Saturday morning, after giving Tiger her breakfast, I told my mother that I would be back by late afternoon, in time, to give Tiger her second meal.

At Anna's house we had a real good time. We swam in her swimming pool, played chess and had lunch in the back lawn.

Then we read for a while sitting under a tree, and had another swim. It was a beautiful summer afternoon and the day was filled with enjoyment. I didn't notice the time. It was late.

Suddenly I realised that it was nearly six o'clock! I quickly said goodbye to Anna and raced home on my bike. When I got home, there was my father playing with the kitten. Everything looked perfectly fine. 'Hi, dad,' I said, 'I'm back!'

'Hello,' he said, 'did you have a nice time?'
I told him what all we had done and how nice it
felt to swim.
'But,' he said, 'you forgot something. You
forgot to give Tiger her meal!'
'I know,' I said, 'I'm sorry. I didn't realise how
late it was.'

'Well, I fed her for you,' said my father. 'And gave her some water in her bowl because she was thirsty too. You had even forgotten to leave her some water before you went.'

'You have been very caring towards Tiger. But you must remember that the pet is your responsibility. If you can't be here to look after her, you have to arrange for someone else who will take care of her. Is that alright?'

I nodded. 'I'm sorry dad. I'll never forget my duty towards Tiger ever. ' And I kept my word.

It is better to try and succeed than not to try at all

Our school's annual sports day was coming
up. A whole day without lessons! We would be
having relay races, bike races, throwing
and jumping competitions. It was going to be a
great day except for one thing.

I really wanted to run in the sprint races but I was never very good at sports. If I participated, I wanted to do well. But I knew that I would not be able to run fast enough. I was worried that I would come last and people would laugh.

My elder brother is good at sports and he had
included his name in lots of events. He said
to me, 'Jamie, come on, you should participate
in the races. Give it a try! I am sure it will be
fun.'

'I'll probably come last,' I said.
'Look, you won't know until you try, will you? It's better to try something and not succeed, than not to try at all! Go on.'
'You think so, really?'
'I know it,' he said and gave me a pat on the back.

I thought about it for some more time. I thought perhaps Jamie was right. The sports day was two weeks away. I could even practise a little before the race. So I started running a little bit each day.

Finally, the day of the race came. It was warm and sunny. The competition began with a speech by the head teacher. Then a parade of the participating pupils took place around the field.

The first events were the jumping and throwing events. I was feeling a bit nervous thinking about the two races I had participated in. But I tried to calm myself by sitting in the shade and watching the jumping event.

Then our turn came. The gun fired and we began running. I had a good start and till halfway I was close to the leaders. At the end of the race I came second last. But I felt great. My friend Brent shook hands and congratulated me.

I looked up to where my parents were sitting and gave them a wave. They clapped in return. My brother came over and congratulated me for giving it a try. I was very glad that I had entered the races.

Then it was time for rest. I sat down and had
a cold drink while I waited for the second race
in which I had entered. This was the 200 metres
race! I was thinking that maybe over the longer
distance I would do better.

We lined up in our lanes. Again there were ten of us in the race. I concentrated on what I had to do. I wasn't as strong as some of the other runners but perhaps if I was careful, I would finish well.

The gun fired and we were off! At the start I was a little behind most of the runners but I increased my speed steadily. As I passed the 100 metre mark, the finish line was in sight. I pushed myself to go faster. I finished in third place!

Later, as we were going home, my father said
'Well done. See, you don't know unless you
try. Hmm, do you think you could beat me in a
race to that ice cream shop?' he said pointing
ahead. The winner gets an ice cream. Off I ran!

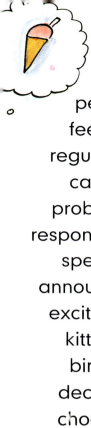

New words

pet	lawn	duty
feed	notice	annual
regularly	beautiful	competition
care	enjoyment	sprint
problem	bike	worried
responsibility	perfectly	participated
spend	thinking	laugh
announced	distance	included
excitedly	metres	succeed
kitten	concentrated	practise
birth	runners	race
decide	increased	sunny
choose	winner	parade
manner	ahead	nervous
remember	beat	watching
starting	realised	calm
invited	goodbye	events
afternoon	nice	congratulated
weekend	forgot	parents
meal	bowl	clapped
chess	forgotten	entered
swam	thirsty	glad
swim	arrange	

What did you learn?

Consequences
What name did the child give to the kitten?
How many meals did the kitten have each day?
Who looked after the kitten when the child was late home?

It is better to try and succeed than not to try at all
Who is Jamie?
How many races did the boy run?
Where did the child and the father run to?